HELLO & BONJOUR
CANADA

TO SAMI, MAX, RYAN, LISA, AND MOM

Written by Amanda Minuk
Assembled and designed by Amanda Minuk
All graphics and images licensed from Canva.com
Contributors include:
Cover: snow (4zevar), Canadian Beaver (Giuseppe Ramos G), Trees (Clker-Free-Vectors-Images from pixaby), Canoe (UoaHH), Trees with snow (PNGWorld), hockey stick and puck (Twemoji), Mountains (All Day April).
Pg. 1 - Maple Leaf (Belle's)
Pg. 3 . Canadian Beaver (Giuseppe Ramos G,)
Pg. 4 Earth (igorkrasnoselkyi)
Pg. 5. Grass and rocks (Procrea), Trees (Open ClipArt from Pixaby) Pine Tree (Nadzin), Mountains (Aleksander), Moose (jemastock), Tents (Eucalyp from amethysstudio), Beaver (Giuseppe Ramos G), Lake (M.Wallflower from Trendify),
Pg. 6 Turtle (Angga Yafi), Maple Leafs (Giuseppe Ramos G)
Pg. 7 Old Paper (C2k2 from High anh cua kien can), Maple Leafs(Giuseppe Ramos G)
Page 8. Toque (Open ClipArt from Pixaby). Beaver (New Wind), Grass (Procrea), Maple Tree (EasyToPrintArt) Canadian Flag (Oleg),
Page 9 Social media UI Frames Quiz (Sparklestroke),
Page 10 Trees (Open ClipArt Vectors from Pixaby), Beaver and building (New Wind), Horse (mybeautifulfiles), Grass (Procrea)
Page 11. Geese (Taras Adamovych), Moose (jemastock), Trees (NinaCliparts from pixabay), Grass (Procrea),
Page 12. Adult skater (Jump Studio), Red Skater (BNPDesignStudio),Green skater (Ksenya Savva), Skating Rink (Ouch! Illustrations), Beaver (New Wind), Trees (Clker-Free-Vectors-Images from pixaby), Basketball Net(DAPA Images), Lacross Stick (Icons8).
Page 13. Cow (Anthony Fever), Poop (Giuseppe Ramos G), Skating Rink (Ouch! Illustrations)
Page 14. Beaver (Giuseppe Ramos G), Beaver Tail (Owren Studio), poutine (Naris Artyuengyong from valueinvestor), Maple Syrup (draftsndoodles), Butter Tarts (BNPDesignStudio), Plate (Retnoutari from GO IDEA),
Page 15. Beaver (Giuseppe Ramos G), Dock (Macrovector), Canoe (UoaHH) Trees (Open ClipArt Vectors from Pixaby), Cabin (DAPA Images), Sun (Nur Rosyitah from MomCreative),
Page 16. Glacier (Sketchify Education), Water (grmarc2), Rock (grmarc2), Shrub (sparkle stroke), Plane (Ianna Rallonza from Sketchify Education),
Page 17. Colourful houses (BNPDesignStudio), water (M.Wallflower from Trendify), Ocean Boats (ixdesignlab), Boat (YummyBuum),
Page 18. Water (grmarc2), Pier (EmilTimplaru), Beaver (New Wind),
Page 19. Trees (Open ClipArt Vectors from Pixaby), Water and Rock (blueringmedia), Canoe (UoaHH), Beaver (New Wind), Goggles (Tive Studio),
Page 20. Lighthouse (Juliars), sunset (Amrtrzk), Whale (BNPDesignStudio), Rock (Open ClipArt Vectors from Pixaby), Water (grmarc2), Beaver (Giuseppe Ramos S).
Page 21. Winter Snow (Natalya Nepran) Penguin skiing and snowboarding(Oleg), Moose snowboarding (DAPA Images), Trees with snow (PNGWorld).
Page 22. Skating Rink (Ouch! Illustrations), Parliament (NotionPic), Skating Bunny (tannikart), Xmas Hat (Superbsub Studio), Beaver Skating (Vintage Illustrations), Beaver (New Wind).
Pg. 23 Toronto Skyline (NotionPic), Car (djvstock), Truck (Sylph Creatives), Red car (stuidiog).
Pg. 24. Snow hills (sketchify), Polar bears (Christana).
Pg. 25 Thatch Grass (Nova Patriot from Nadzieja Porto), birds (solitons).
Pg. 26. Mountains (All Day April), Trees (Open ClipArt Vectors from Pixaby), Beaver (Giuseppe Ramos S), Canoe (UoaHH), Rocks (YummyBuum), Fossil (luisline).
Page 27. Tent (Addinaimada), Beaver (Giuseppe Ramos S and Canadian Beaver Giuseppe Ramos G), Stars (grmarc). Horse (pat stairhead from pat's team), Fences (writerfantast and Nanchaikan).
Page 28. Beavers (New Wind), Mountains (Sketchify Korea), Log (Lera Feeva), Bicycle (harshal07 from pixaby), Sunscreen (graphixmania), bucket hat (blueringmedia), flag (Clker-Free-Vector-Images from Pixaby).
Page 29. Mountains (All Day April), Chair lift (Smashing Stocks from Vectors Market), Trees (PNGWorld)Marmot (Olha Saiuk).
Page 30. Grass and shrub(Procrea), Log Cabin with tree (Open Clipart-Vectors from pixaby), Bear (blueringmedia), Elk (Magtira Paolo from Sketchify Education), Canadian flag (Oleg).
Page 31. Northern Lights (Gluiki).
Page 32. Snow (Dhananach), Inukshuk (heyrabbiticons).

ISBN 978-1-990730-27-6 Hardcover
For wholesale inquiries reach out to amanda@doodlepawpress.com

Copyright 2023 Doodle Paw Press

All rights reserved.
No part of this publication may be reproduced, stored in a retrieval system, or transmitted in any form or by any means, electronic, mechanical, photocopying, recording or otherwise, without written permission of the publisher.

HELLO & BONJOUR
CANADA

BY: AMANDA MINUK

Hello and bonjour to Canada!
That's the really big country on the top of North America.

DID YOU KNOW?
Canada is the 2nd largest country in the world and has two official languages- English and French.

HOW DID CANADA GET ITS NAME?

Canada comes from the Indigenous word "kanata", meaning "settlement" or "village".

DID YOU KNOW?
In 1535, two Indigenous youths told European explorer, Jacques Cartier, about the route to "kanata". They were referring to a village near present day Quebec City, but Cartier used the word to describe the entire area.

DID YOU KNOW?
Some Indigenous people refer to North America as Turtle Island. According to various Indigenous oral histories, the turtle is believed to be part of earth's creation story.

There was actually a debate about what to name the country. The list below includes all the names that were being considered.

Possible Country Names:

- Albionora
- Albertsland
- Borealia
- Victoria Land
- Brittania
- Tuponia
- Cabotia
- Efisga
- Colonia
- Hochelega
- Norland
- Canada
- Superior

Can you imagine being a Cabotian or a Tuponian? Which name would you pick?

DID YOU KNOW?
Canada became a new country on July 1st, 1867.

CANADIANA TRIVIA AND FUN FACTS!

FUN FACT

The maple leaf has been an important symbol for Canada since the early 1800s, but the Canadian flag- as we know it today- wasn't finalized until 1965 after years of debate and thousands of designs.

DID YOU KNOW?

Canada's official national colours are red and white.

If you had to pick a symbol and colours to represent your house what would you pick?

THE ANSWER IS:

The beaver and horse!

WHY THE BEAVER?

Fur hats were very popular in Europe in the late 1600s and early 1700s, earning Canada a lot of money from selling beaver fur. Beavers almost went extinct from how much fur was being sold!

DID YOU KNOW?

There's a Canadian horse breed called the "Canadian Horse". It was given national animal status in 2002.

The moose and the goose are symbolic of Canada, but they are NOT Canada's national animals.

DID YOU KNOW?
Canada has the largest moose population in the world.

DID YOU KNOW?
The plural of moose is moose but the plural of goose is geese.

WHY ARE THE NATIONAL POLICE CALLED "MOUNTIES"?

- **A** BECAUSE THEY RIDE BICYCLES FOR PATROL.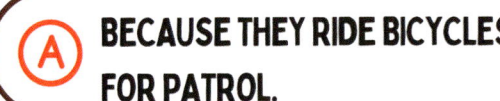
- **B** BECAUSE THEY RIDE HORSES FOR PATROL.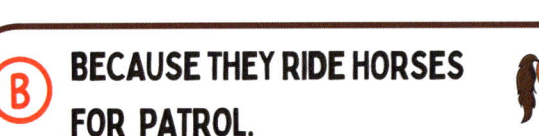
- **C** BECAUSE THEY HAVE MOUNTAINS ON THEIR UNIFORMS.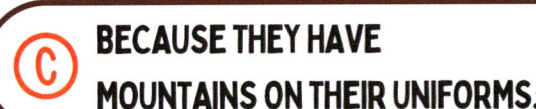
- **D** BECAUSE THEY ARE EXPERT MOUNTAIN RESCUERS.

DID YOU KNOW?

The Royal Northwest Mounted Police (then became Royal Canadian Mounted Police) was created in 1873 to protect Canada's north western frontier from lawlessness in the Wild West.

THE ANSWER IS...

B. "Mounties" became a nickname for the police because they rode on horseback. The term "mounted" refers to the act of sitting on a horse.

CANADIAN INVENTIONS

Canadians have been responsible for adding these inventions to the world: Insulin, walkie-talkies, the snowblower, the egg carton and the electric wheelchair.

DID YOU KNOW?

The inventor of the telephone, Alexander Graham Bell, was not technically Canadian, but Canada played a big role in his life and the invention of the telephone. It's believed the world's "first long distance call" (one-way only) was made between his place in Brantford, Ontario to Paris, Ontario on August 10, 1876.

HOCKEY, EH.

Hockey is Canada's official winter sport. While the game of hockey wasn't invented in Canada, Canadians are responsible for modernizing and evolving the sport to what it is today.

FUN FACT

Canada also has an official summer sport- lacrosse. Lacrosse was invented by Indigenous people.

DID YOU KNOW?

Basketball was invented by a Canadian in the year 1891.

FUN FACT

The first hockey pucks were not like we know it today. Some of the earliest pucks are believed to have been made with frozen cow poop and only lasted one game. Stinky!

DID YOU KNOW?

The 1st organized hockey game was played in Montreal in 1875. The teams played using a flat, wooden block.

CANADIAN FOODS

Canadians have invented some yummy foods including: Poutine, butter tarts, nanaimo bars, beaver tails, ketchup chips, peanut butter and Hawaiian pizza.

"Don't worry you're not really eating my tail. A "beaver tail" is a fried pastry, like a flat donut."

DID YOU KNOW?
Indigenous people were the first to make maple syrup- which involves taking sap from a Maple tree.

FUN FACT
Canada produces 75-85% of the world's maple syrup.

What's your favourite food to put maple syrup on?

LAKE LIFE

Canada has the most lakes in the entire world with approximately two million lakes.

FUN FACT
Canada has three ocean coasts- the Atlantic to the east, the Pacific to the West and the Arctic to the North.

Let's go on a tour of Canada- where have you been so far?

HELLO NEWFOUNDLAND AND LABRADOR!

The easternmost province, on the edge of North America, is Newfoundland and Labrador. Newfoundland is known for its friendly culture, natural beauty and fishing history.

FUN FACT
It's pronounced "New-fin-luhnd".

FUN FACT
This province is one and a half hours ahead of Eastern Standard Time. So if it's 10:00am in Ontario, it's 11:30am in Newfoundland.

DID YOU KNOW?
St. John's is the oldest city in Canada. It is known for having colourful houses.

FUN FACT
In 2022, the oldest gold coin was discovered on a beach in Newfoundland. The coin dates back to the 1420s.

HELLO PRINCE EDWARD ISLAND!

Known for its red soil, beautiful beaches, yummy potatoes and lobsters, PEI is the smallest and only province you can bike or run from tip to tip.

FUN FACT

PEI's Confederation Trail is 449KM of multipurpose trail- great for running, walking or biking. That distance would take ~30 hours of nonstop biking! *What's the longest you've ever biked, walked or ran?*

BONJOUR NEW BRUNSWICK!

The world's biggest tides can be found in the Bay of Fundy. Because the tides are so high, rocks have changed shape to form beautiful formations.

FUN FACT
Hopewell Rocks in New Brunswick are one of the the most famous rock formations to see.

DID YOU KNOW?
New Brunswick is officially a bilingual province. Bilingual means two languages.

HELLO NOVA SCOTIA!

Nova Scotia, Latin for "New Scotland", is on the Atlantic Ocean and is known for its maritime history, epic scenic drives, beautiful beaches and lighthouses.

DID YOU KNOW?

Peggy's Cove is the most photographed lighthouse in the world. Nova Scotia also has the most lighthouses in Canada.

FUN FACT

Cape Breton is an island part of Nova Scotia. It has the Cabot Trail, a famous 298 km (roughly 5-6 hour drive) roadway that takes you along the coast.

BONJOUR QUÉBEC !

Québec is the only province with French as its sole official language and is known for its vibrant Québecois culture. Québec is home to the Laurentian mountains and is the biggest producer of maple syrup in the country.

FUN FACT
Québec City is the 2nd oldest city in Canada. The city still has its defensive walls and is a UNESCO World Heritage Site.

DID YOU KNOW?
The ski mountain 'Mont Tremblant' comes from the Algonquin Indigenous people who called the mountain the "trembling mountain". They believed the wilderness god would throw rocks when it was upset, causing the mountain to tremble.

HELLO ONTARIO!

Ottawa is Canada's capital city, and where the Prime Minister and Parliament are located.

DID YOU KNOW?
In the winter, Ottawa's Rideau Canal turns into the world's largest skating rink- 7.8 km. It would take 1-2 hours to skate.

Toronto is the most populous city in Canada and has one of the largest free standing structures in the world.

CN TOWER

FUN FACT
The co-creator of Superman was from Toronto.

FUN FACT
Niagara Falls is less than a two hour drive from Toronto and is the most powerful waterfall in the world.

FUN FACT
Toronto's Yonge Street is the longest street in the world- 56 km. It would take almost 12 hours to walk.

HELLO MANITOBA!

Manitoba is one of the prairie provinces, with snowy, cold winters and warm summer weather.

DID YOU KNOW?
The Forks, in Winnipeg, is where the Red and Assiniboine rivers meet. The grounds has been a meeting place for more than 6,000 years and currently a wonderful space to visit.

FUN FACT
Winnipeg's famous intersection at Portage and Main is known as the "windiest corner" in the country.

FUN FACT
Churchill, Manitoba is known as "the polar bear" capital of the world- Canada has 60% of the world's polar bears.

What sound do you think a polar bear makes?

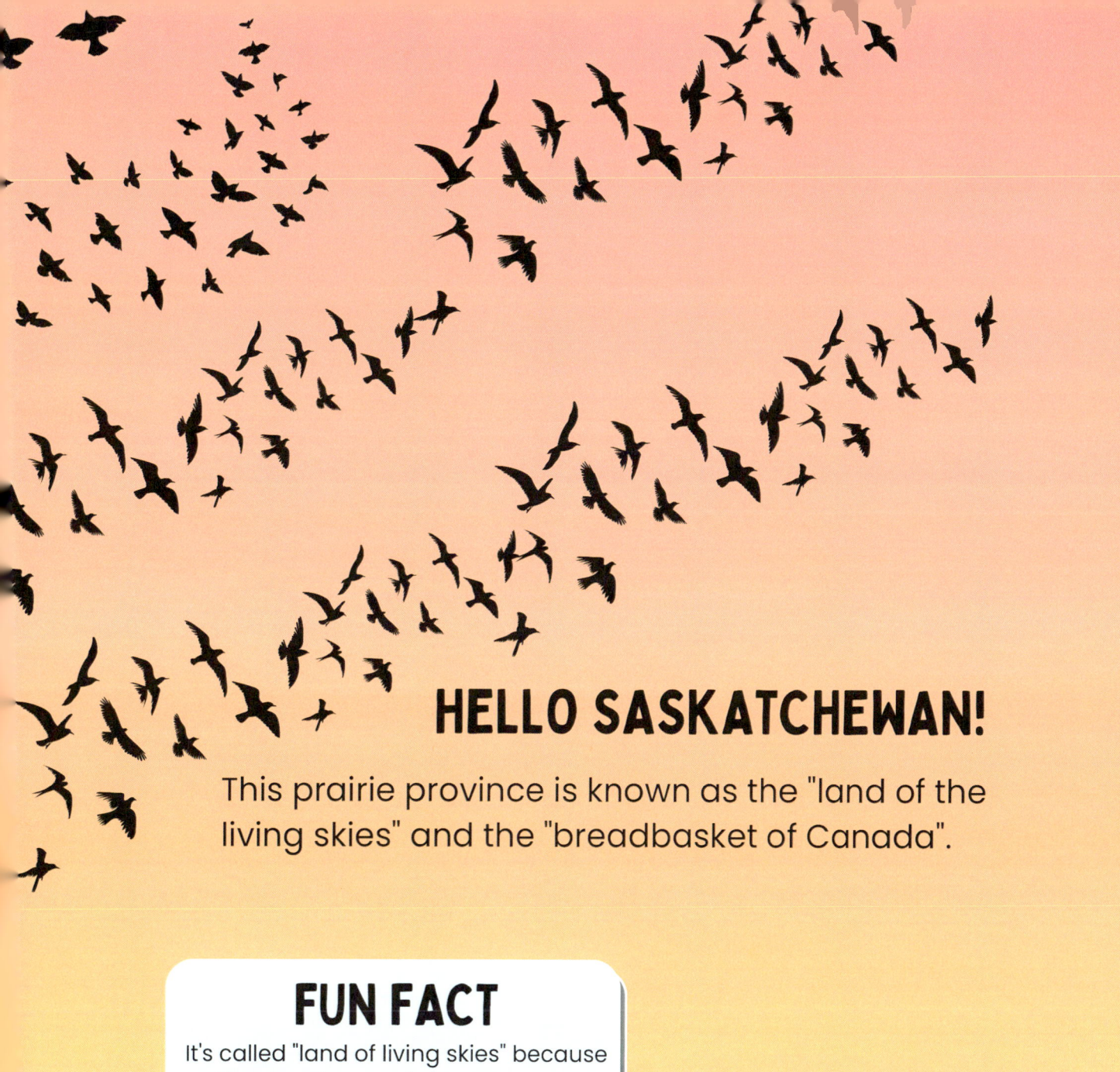

HELLO SASKATCHEWAN!

This prairie province is known as the "land of the living skies" and the "breadbasket of Canada".

FUN FACT
It's called "land of living skies" because of its stunning sunrises and sunsets.

DID YOU KNOW?
In spring and fall, thousands of birds can be seen migrating.

DID YOU KNOW?
It's called "breadbasket" because of the many wheat fields (to make bread :).

HELLO ALBERTA!

Alberta is one of the most picturesque provinces with snow peaked Rocky Mountains, stunning lakes, and amazing provincial parks.

FUN FACT

Banff National Park is Canada's oldest national park, established in 1885. Banff's Lake Louise is one of the most photographed lakes in the world.

DID YOU KNOW?

Alberta has a Dinosaur Provincial Park, home to some of the most important dinosaur fossils. It is a UNESCO World Heritage Site.

FUN FACT
The superhero Wolverine is from Alberta, Canada.

DID YOU KNOW?
Jasper National Park is a "blackout" park where no artificial lights are allowed.

DID YOU KNOW?
The first Calgary Stampede took place in 1912 and occurs every year in July.

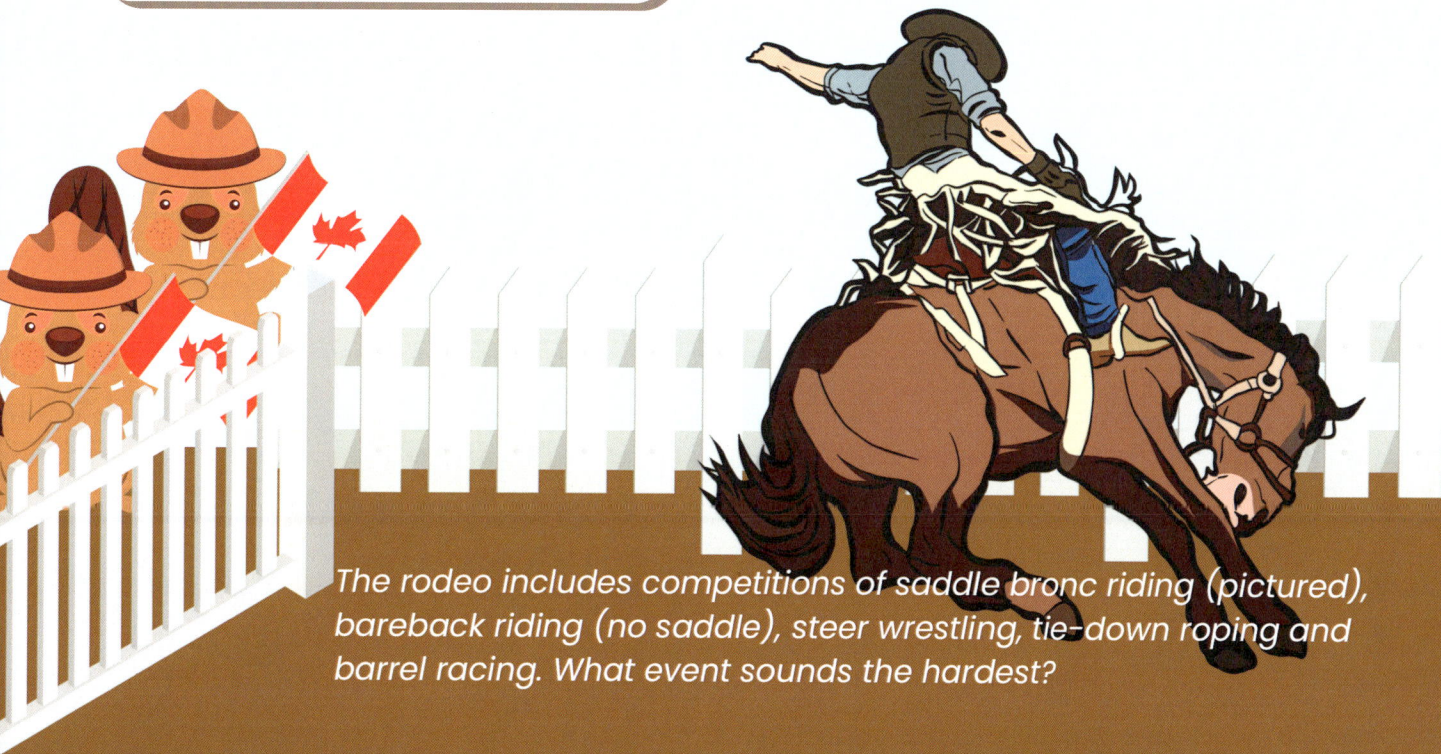

The rodeo includes competitions of saddle bronc riding (pictured), bareback riding (no saddle), steer wrestling, tie-down roping and barrel racing. What event sounds the hardest?

HELLO BRITISH COLUMBIA!

British Columbia (BC) is located on the Pacific coast and is the most westerly province. BC is a popular destination for its outdoor activities of skiing, hiking and surfing.

FUN FACT
BC has ~25,725 km of coastline.

DID YOU KNOW?
Vancouver's Stanley Park is over 1000 acres and bigger than New York's Central Park. Stanley Park has two beaches and a Seawall which you can bike on while looking at the ocean.

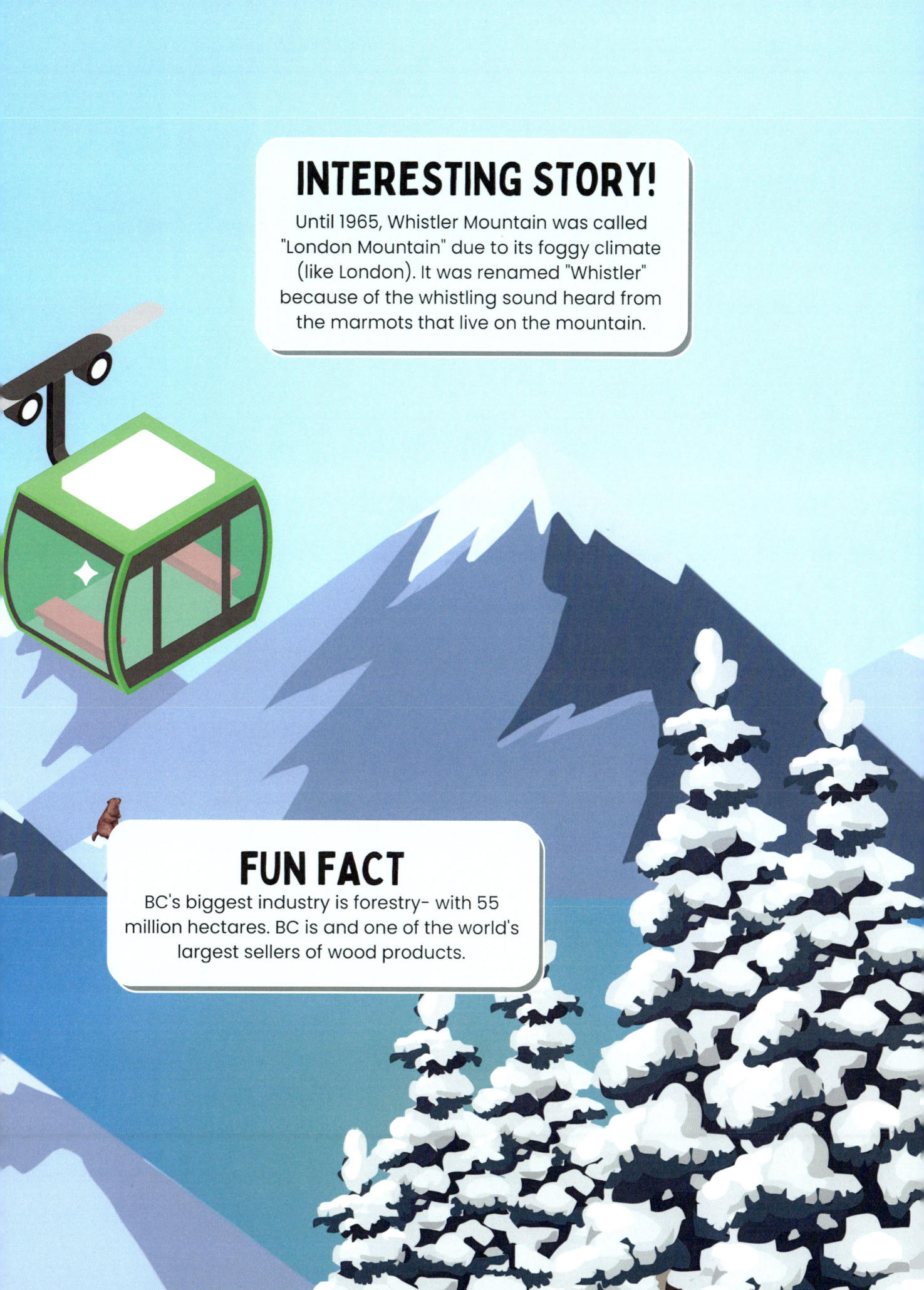

INTERESTING STORY!

Until 1965, Whistler Mountain was called "London Mountain" due to its foggy climate (like London). It was renamed "Whistler" because of the whistling sound heard from the marmots that live on the mountain.

FUN FACT

BC's biggest industry is forestry- with 55 million hectares. BC is and one of the world's largest sellers of wood products.

HELLO YUKON!

The Yukon is a territory in Canada known for its wilderness and made famous from the Klondike Gold Rush. The Yukon is home to distinct wildlife like moose, elk, caribou and grizzly bears.

DID YOU KNOW?
In 1896 gold was found in the Klondike region of the Yukon Territories. Many people went there to find gold, causing the famous "gold rush".

FUN FACT
The lowest temperature ever recorded in Canada was -62.8°C in Snag, Yukon.

HELLO NORTHWEST TERRITORIES!

Northwest Territories is a northern territory in Canada's Arctic, known for its nature, rich Indigenous history and stunning Northern Lights.

FUN FACT

The Northern Lights, also known as Aurora Borealis, is a phenomenon in the sky. It appears as if the lights are dancing. The best viewing is in the winter of the Northwest Territories.

DID YOU KNOW?

In the summer there are 24 hours of sun and in the winter there are 24 hours of darkness.

HELLO NUNAVUT!

Nunavut is Canada's newest and and most northern territory on the Arctic coast. Nunavut means "our land" in Inuktitut, the Inuit language.

DID YOU KNOW?
An inukshuk is an Inuit stone landmark made by stacking rocks in a specific way. The word "inukshuk" means "in the likeness of a person" in the Inuit language. Inukshuks are built to guide travellers, warn of danger, and mark important places.

DID YOU KNOW?
In 1999, The Northwest Territories was split into two, enabling the Inuit people to have their own government and home.

CANADIANISMS

CANADIAN SLANG AND TERMS ONLY CANADIANS USE:

Eh- An expression added to the end of a sentence to make it into a question, "you know, eh?".

Toque- A winter hat.

For sure- Definitely, yes.

Mountie- A member of the Royal Canadian Mounted Police (RCMP).

Loonie- A one dollar coin (a loon is pictured on the 1 dollar coin).

Toonie- A two dollar coin (combination of two+loonie).

The 6ix- Refers to the cities that make up Toronto.

Pop- Soda or soft drink.

Washroom - The term for bathroom, toilets, or the loo.

Runners-Running/comfortable shoes to wear, like sneakers.

Snowbird- Canadians who travel south for the winter.

Cottage/cabin/lake house- The name for a vacation home.

Canuck-Nickname for a Canadian person.

Great White North- Nickname for the country (Great-big size, White -Arctic and snow; North- our location).

Are we missing any? Let us know @doodlepawpress

MAP OF CANADA

There's so much more to each province, territory and country than written in this book! That just means you'll have to visit each of the 10 provinces and 3 territories to learn more. Colour in the provinces you want to visit!

www.ingramcontent.com/pod-product-compliance
Lightning Source LLC
Chambersburg PA
CBRC091205010526
44107CB00021B/1251